NLP

The Use Of Covert Methods Of Influence, Mind Control, Covert Manipulation, And Neuro-linguistic Programming, Consider The Behavior Of Humans And Steer Clear Of Manipulation

(One Of The Most Important Books For Novices, This Guide Will Explain The Secrets Behind Mind Control)

BeslanMorozova

TABLE OF CONTENT

Some Standard Techniques Used In Dark Psychology..1

Relationship Between NLP Techniques And Learning Capacity..13

Rephrasing Content And Shifting Beliefs..........36

What NLP Is For..63

Utilising Internal Representations To Captivate People's Imagination 74

Managing The Suffering Caused By Strained Relationships... 109

Some Standard Techniques Used In Dark Psychology

You can rely on various strategies while working with dark psychology to get the desired outcomes. This will make the procedure more difficult to work with. Therefore, we'll break it down into three primary methods most effective in dark psychology. These consist of persuasion, empathy, and manipulation. Let's explore these facets in more detail so that we can use dark psychology to help you reach your objectives and get amazing outcomes.

Managing

When we deal with dark psychology, the concept of manipulation will be the first method we encounter. A lot of individuals are already terrified of this and believe that if someone did it to them in real life, they would be able to identify it. Perhaps they think it will be the same since they have seen many books and movies about evil manipulation. These media tend to sensationalize these issues, and you will discover that manipulating people in real life is harder than it seems in movies and books. Nobody would be able to carry out the manipulation, and it would not be added to the list of dark psychology techniques if it were as simple to spot as what we see on TV. Without this happening to them, everyone would have known when they would be deceived and be prepared to leave. What would motivate the manipulator to keep working hard if this were the case? Those skilled at manipulating people will be far more adept at doing it without being discovered. There are numerous circumstances in which manipulation will go on for years. Even if the manipulator is the one pulling the strings all the time, the objective still requires that they have the power to decide for themselves and behave as they like. Firstly, it is important to examine the nature of this manipulation and the reasons it warrants consideration in the context of dark psychology. When we discuss dark manipulation, we primarily mean the attempt to manipulate the selected target's perceptions, actions, and behaviors by subtle and deceitful means. To make sure the goal accomplishes what the manipulator wants, they will fabricate tales, lie, and take any necessary actions. Dark manipulation frequently results in injury to the target. They will get along with the manipulator because they believe it is in their best interest, even though they may later deceive the target. When using dark manipulation, the manipulator's primary concern is how they may advance their interests and realize their objectives. The target will frequently sustain damage as a result of the process. They're going to be an instrument. They will find that they are harmed in the process and do not get anything from this relationship with the manipulator, regardless of whether they are mentally, physically, or emotionally hurt.

Furthermore, as long as the manipulator can achieve their goals, it doesn't matter how the target is hurt. When we examine persuasion, some methods utilized in manipulation will also be comparable. They will consist of lying or withholding information, trickery, guilt trips, humiliation, censure, victimization by the manipulator, and more. The takeaway is that, with the victim's assistance, the manipulator will employ any strategy, no matter how cunning and immoral, to help them get the desired outcomes and accomplish their ultimate objectives.

Convincing

There are numerous situations in which persuasion will be employed. When believing in business, we can see that it's a process that influences how an individual or group behaves toward a particular thing, another individual, idea, thing, or event. They can accomplish this through written, verbal, and visual aids. Persuasion is not limited to companies; it may also be applied in other contexts. Additionally, you can utilize belief to further your interests or achieve personal success. We may see it in an election campaign or when someone makes a great sales pitch to us. Persuasion may also be employed to interpret one's own or position's resources to influence the actions or viewpoints of others.

As you can see, there are a variety of applications for persuasion, each slightly distinct from the other. However, you'll find that several research studies employ comparable methods to get the same outcomes. What distinguishes conventional persuasion from dark persuasion, then?

I'll go into more depth regarding persuasion and its mechanisms later, but the other person's purpose greatly matters. Both will use techniques to achieve their aims, but it all depends on whether or not they plan to harm the other person or purpose. The target will continue to hold most of the power with consistent persuasion. I have the freedom to follow your beliefs or not. Usually, it will be advantageous to both parties. The persuader is aware that they will benefit from the agreement. However, they also understand that the target won't suffer any harm when they succeed. They will still be free to choose, benefiting both parties. We can now discuss what is referred to as "dark persuasion." Many of the same strategies used in other forms of persuasion can also be applied to this kind of belief, albeit the goal and objective will be slightly different. It is common for certain techniques that are not as effective as others, and whether or not the target is harmed in the process is irrelevant to the persuader. The objective of the persuader is to achieve their desired outcome and state of affairs. It doesn't matter to them if someone else is harmed in the process. They don't give a damn if the other person has hurt their feelings or suffered psychological harm or even bodily harm as a result. They will be satisfied with the outcomes if they see things through and accomplish their objectives.

Empathy

The final method we'll look at is the application of empathic knowledge to dark psychology. When we hear empathy and empathy, we automatically assume that the other person is kind and compassionate and always thinking about what's best for them. This is a wonderful perspective on life, but just because you can tell when someone is ill, joyful, or experiencing other emotions doesn't mean you must take that information to heart. Why not make use of those feelings to your advantage? It's not always a negative thing to be an empath, even if you're trying to employ some dark psychological tactics. Many people believe that when we grow in empathy and empathy, we have to talk about the appropriate topic. We are discussing the kind of person more sensitive to the sentiments and emotions of those around them, so shouldn't it be put to good use? Naturally, a lot of empaths will always use this ability. They'll discover how to use it to improve their interpersonal relationships and ability to be present for others. What if you could advocate for the world's objectives and the visions you wish to have for yourself using the thoughts that arise from being an empath?

The boundaries of who can be an empath and when they can come out have been defined by society for a long time. When an empath refuses to repress their feelings during an awkward situation, we advise them to quit being so sensitive and make fun of them. We discover that we ask them to come out when we need someone to lean on or who is good with a variety of people, and we become angry when they say they are too busy or don't know how to do it. Similar to an individual. Why not take the concept of being an empath and use it to our advantage rather than allowing others to dictate who we are and how we should respond to certain situations? Similar viewpoints apply, and you can use empathy to feel other people's feelings and accomplish your goals simultaneously. This will be terrific in your life since you may learn about other people's emotions and know exactly what they think and feel. For instance, you are more likely to know who to target when manipulating and convincing someone. You can swiftly determine whether someone will fit into your strategy or if you should go on to someone else because you are aware of that person's feelings. As an empath, you'll frequently be able to sense whether someone will provide you with the energy you require. You can feel the feelings of others around you and select the ideal companions for yourself (whose emotions you can comprehend much more readily because of your special abilities as an empath). Those who exude energy, pleasure, and enjoyment are prepared to go above and beyond to ensure you have the same qualities. Alternatively, you may want to take it a step further and resolve to harness the energy of those in your immediate vicinity to ensure that you don't experience regret or guilt about your actions with this individual. Maybe we all carry a little bit of dark psychology within us. However, you could discover that it is a little harder for you not to take on guilt or any associated feelings of dread, worry, grief, or whatever else arises from using these strategies if you are an empath. You can work with someone who will take on some of those feelings rather than listen to them and give up some of the strategies and objectives you want to pursue. This helps eliminate unwanted negative emotions, yet it might also be another empath or someone you would like to collaborate with. As you can see, an empath can be anything you desire despite the stereotypes society has created about those who possess this ability. This may be used to work with dark psychology as much as you'd want if you're prepared to put in the work and would like to know more about empathic abilities and their advantages.

Relationship Between NLP Techniques And Learning Capacity

Humanity will always seek to learn more; this is no different than humanity's efforts to improve the knowledge they have already gained. And as previously indicated, this may be explained by the fact that education is a way of life.

Unfortunately, learning is sometimes misunderstood to be restricted to a process involving a great deal of thinking and the development and enhancement of an individual's intellectual faculties alone. However, the reality is that education affects every other facet of life. When we study, we not only get information, but we also become aware of our potential. We often push ourselves over our comfort zones to see how far we can push ourselves. Learning is the process by which we not only gain knowledge but also participate in self-discovery and self-examination, leading to the full development of our personalities.

Since its introduction as a cutting-edge method of instruction, neuro-linguistic programming techniques rank among the most suitable and successful approaches to higher-level, more in-depth learning. Not only can NLP help people develop their behavioral side, but it also encourages them to use reason rationally and analytically. Consequently, knowledge is gained, and what has been acquired is fully understood.

To sum up, to achieve one's life goals, one must immerse oneself in learning and maintain a healthy balance between intellectual capacity, emotional stability, and an optimistic personality. These are all very important factors required to achieve one's potential and further improve and accelerate one's learning capacity. And these could be accomplished with the help of a novel school of thought: the methods of neuro-linguistic programming.

Section Four

NLP Metaprograms: You need to understand fundamental mindset patterns to gain insight into your potential clientele's thoughts.

First of all,

Selling an established product with a fresh approach is challenging in the modern era of fiercely competitive corporate environments and diverse consumer opinions. Problems include handling insufficient skills and suitable reaction mechanisms that impede sellers' advancement, leading to disheartened and ineffective responses. NLP Meta-programs can be used in these situations to support the approaches taken and offer effective solutions for problems involving higher technical standards. This will give sellers the tools they need to meet the demands of the current obstacles and get a competitive edge over their rivals, in addition to developing mechanisms to connect with the buyer and ensure success in selling the good or service. This How-To guide aims to define and elucidate Meta-programs that can significantly boost productivity and facilitate the sale of any kind of product to a customer.

What is the need for NLP Meta-programs?

Neuro-Linguistic Programming, or NLP , is a specialized technique that studies behavioral patterns and character analysis. Selling is using unique buyer characteristics to market goods and services. This involves understanding NLP meta-programs in selling. It entails improvising how to interact with potential clients by paying close attention to even the smallest shifts in their behavioral patterns and acting accordingly to get the intended outcomes. Selecting among a variety of NLP meta-programs requires in-depth comprehension and sufficient knowledge. When used effectively, these strategies can significantly contribute to salespeople's personal and professional development. Businesses dealing with a big clientele might benefit from meta-programs and achieve more assured and favorable results with prospective customers. The first step in selecting patterns and meta-molds for each type of buyer is determining which meta-program is best for them.

What you should understand before starting an NLP Meta-program:

Before moving further with the many kinds of meta-programs to obtain a more thorough understanding of the overview of this approach, there are a few important things to be aware of. The goal is to be ready to handle any circumstance—planned or unforeseen—comfortably. The purpose of the following recommendations is to give a quick overview of the fundamentals of the meta-program.

First and foremost, it is crucial to remember that the theory of meta-programs incorporated several real-world experiences and placed more emphasis on the use of informational tools than on scholarly or scientific methods.

Second, inflexible personality type classifications and metaprogramme ideas will only stifle original thought. It is important to realize that purchasers possess many different qualities—they are not limited to extremes. Usually, a middle ground has to be given the same consideration.

Thirdly, astute observation, strong intuition, and absorption of all psychological features are essential for ongoing development and modification. Each merchant is allowed to customize the current methods.

Fourthly, to produce a fair meta-program analysis, find the ideal balance between remaining professional and establishing a rapport with the customer. Overtly formal behavior can limit the buyer's flexibility, but too much friendliness can undermine the seller's objectivity.

Finally, it is necessary to make adjustments and shifts in strategy during the communication process to respond quickly to any pertinent information the customer discloses.

Repeated phrases

Repetitive Word Examples: once more, anyway, additionally, and back

The benefit of using repetitive words is that they let the reader or listener instinctively visualize the same event happening twice, which helps to emphasize the point you're attempting to make.

15.) A large number of my clients return time and time.

This is a complex sentence since it assumes that you have a large clientele that returns time and time. Although it doesn't state it clearly, your audience will infer there must be a compelling reason why they keep returning. Since that would just require a single visit, it cannot be to obtain a refund. They have to be getting something of value from your goods.

16.) Authorities have discovered that this product offers an additional advantage.

Authorities? Who knows? Even if you don't say anything, your readers will conjure up an image that resonates with them and lends credibility to your goods. It is assumed by using "also found" that these "authorities" have already discovered the initial benefit. When it comes to all these, the reader's subconscious uses their imagination to fill in the blank and takes these assumptions as gospel.

17.) You have two options: buy now and never worry about prices again, or search elsewhere for a more expensive product.

Thus, this assumes that your product is the most affordable because if they look at it, they'll only find more expensive options. Additionally, you're assuming their issues will be resolved when they purchase today. This implies that those more expensive products won't even come close to solving their problems; instead, they may either waste time searching around hoping to find nothing, or they can purchase your product immediately and end their issue.

Characteristics

Qualifiers Examples: just, except, even, and only

Qualifiers are excellent for creating fictitious barriers and then breaching them, amplifying your message's impact.

18.) There isn't a monthly charge, so you only have to pay once.

You simply have to pay once for most of the items you purchase. However, this gives the impression that it's a bonus.

20.) You won't find a better product than this unless you decide to develop one yourself.

This example assumes that your product is the greatest available. They probably don't want to make their own as they're actually shopping for a product. Since you have already produced this product, they may assume you possess the knowledge and abilities even though you may not have them. Furthermore, you have to be among the most talented individuals in your field to produce the greatest product, as people have unconsciously considered it the best one available.

Words That Change With Time

Change of Time Word Examples: start, finish, halt, start, continue, already

Words that change time mesmerize the reader because they make them see something that will happen in the future and then start to wonder how it will lead to something else. We naturally love to daydream and allow our imaginations to run wild, so it's difficult to resist either.

21.) You'll be happy you purchased this product once you understand its full potential!

This statement assumes they have previously purchased the substance and know its potency. This also makes people look forward, envisioning how delighted they will be when they buy your goods since it eases their problems. This is extremely hypnotic because they are visualizing the future and letting their mind fill in the blanks.

The past tense of "you'll be glad you bought it" is evident. They will, therefore, be considering beginning a project in the future, but when that time comes, they will be happy that they had (past tense) purchased your product. This is an extremely hypnotic statement because of the several displayed layers.

22.) Many people are still using this product for different things.

How many individuals? Who knows how many people are utilizing the product— your reader will have to speculate. "Continue to use it" implies that they have already used it and that, given their repeated use, it must be an excellent product. A product with a range of uses sounds even more special because it implies that others are utilizing it for uses you may not have even considered or intended!

23.) A few of my most recent clients have already expressed how much better their lives have become.

This example assumes that you have a large number of clients, both current and potential. It assumes that you are well-known and have been in the game for some time. Additionally, a few new clients have already told you how much better their lives are, which is surprising given how quickly it happened.

The idea is that your product is the only reason their lives are so much better. How and why do their lives seem better? The reader will have to speculate as to why. This statement also suggests you communicate directly and consistently with your clients and pay attention to their input. This puts potential clients at ease and encourages them to purchase because they know they can contact you anytime.

24.) Most of the time, folks just go straight to the buy button when they discover how helpful this is.

This statement assumes that you sell many goods, that your customers are quick to make purchases, and that your product is valuable. This offers social proof that not only do a large number of individuals use and enjoy the product, but the majority of others who are reading about it (as they are) also purchase it rapidly. Your readers will, therefore, feel left behind if they don't purchase it immediately. We instinctively avoid circumstances in which we are outsiders or in opposition to a group since we prefer to be welcomed and a part of the group.

Part II: Anchoring

Just for a moment, picture yourself sitting at the kitchen counter with a tray full of freshly baked cookies. The scent of cookie dough fills the entire house; the heat from the oven clings to the tile, and a fleeting glance at the display tray tells you that the chocolate chips haven't cooled down to room temperature yet and are still incredibly sticky. Your mouth waters at one glance.

What thoughts did this provoke in you? Maybe it brought back memories of summers spent as a child at your grandparents' place. Maybe you were raised in a bakery and were reminded to assist your parents in running the company as soon as you were old enough to be left alone and not devour the goods. Alternatively, it might have evoked nothing specific but a hazy memory of an unspecified holiday. Whichever way you feel, there are two important things to remember. Firstly, if you remember anything from this circumstance, it's likely that the aroma of freshly baked cookies is a memory or anchor in your life. If not, it is merely another sensory experience that has no greater significance for you than the majority of other sensory experiences; it is not an anchor. Second, pause to consider the range of mental images that people might generate in addition to those mentioned above; none of them are inherently connected to the scent of freshly made cookies for most people, but for that person, they would be strongly attached. This is the anchoring power: the capacity of an entirely inconspicuous stimulus to entwine itself with a wide range of feelings and mental images.

An anchor is anything that brings back a memory, feeling, or habit. It could be a scent that evokes memories of your grandma, a song that takes you back to your first romantic relationship, or even an ice cream truck that resembles the one you used to chase down the street every day as a youngster. Although they can be useful instruments in our pursuit of happiness, anchors can also be painful emotional baggage that brings up memories of our past. We all already carry a variety of anchors, many of which we are not even aware of. To use NLP to liberate ourselves from emotional baggage and create possibilities to enhance our happiness and success, it is essential to become aware of these anchors.

The Making of Anchors

Anchors are formed when a strong stimulus and a powerful event are combined. It should be noted that anchors match one's favoredsubmodality, though not always. When her partner proposes, she is more likely to pay attention to the radio playing in the adjacent room if she is an auditory learner. Even so, when she receives an email announcing that she has been awarded a much sought-after promotion, the taste of the apple she eats can still serve as a potent anchor.

Although we generally can't stop anchors from forming in intensely emotional situations, it's vital to identify the anchors we carry and assess whether they can harm our well-being. Recognizing chances to enhance our well-being with intentionally designed anchors is equally important.

Rephrasing Content And Shifting Beliefs

There's an innate propensity to respond adversely when something doesn't go our way—for example, when we don't win a competition, get promoted, or in general. However, when objects play a significant beneficial role in our lives, we tend to grow attached to them and see them as a source of happiness and self-worth. The risk associated with either of these situations is permitting our state of being to become dependent on factors outside of our control and become tied to external circumstances. Centuries ago, the esteemed Stoic thinkers, including Epictetus, Seneca the Younger, and emperor Marcus Aurelius, realized this. They created stoicism, a useful method of redefining how the mind views the outside world. They believed that we are always responsible for how we respond to the environment. They were among the first people to use NLP .

Events and things don't always have intrinsic meaning. These things take on meaning for us according to our values, beliefs, and experiences. Depending on one's beliefs about the afterlife, the meaning of death, and even whether it is right or wrong to have a family member taken away, people may react to the loss of a family member in very different ways. A high-end sports vehicle might come to represent a fundamental aspect of our self-worth; at that point, anything that diminishes the car's value also diminishes us, and losing the vehicle means losing a part of who we are. We could quickly criticize ourselves based on how well we perform on an exam or in an interview, and doing poorly can cause our self-worth and self-esteem to plummet. A crucial and effective use of NLP in each of these situations is the capacity to reframe an event by removing the overpoweringly negative elements and substituting them with neutral or positive elements.

The advantages of mastering efficient rephrasing are immense. Reframing is taking command of your journey. It's about maintaining composure in the face of difficulty, rising to the occasion, and maintaining a positive attitude even when those around you start to lose their minds or panic.

Unsurprisingly, realizing that you can alter your response to the outside world is the most crucial first step. It's to realize that your automatic responses are just the result of your innate psychological and biological tendencies and that this initial result is no different from an initial draft of an email. After it's created, you can change it by adding new paragraphs, removing unnecessary ones, or even starting over.

The most effective way to reframe your response to a situation is to create a list of go-to questions that compel you to look at the situation differently. You must start by considering if your response was necessary and prepare yourself to look for other options. Asking yourself, "What is the benefit of my current reaction in this scenario?" is one technique to accomplish this. Is there a chance that this response will have an impact on the scenario's unfavorable aspect?" You'll most likely answer "none" and "no" to these questions, respectively.

After you've admitted that there's no point in wallowing in your misery and that it will probably not solve the real issue, you may start posing questions that will guide you toward developing other responses. Here are a few instances:

"What are the positive outcomes I can find in this scenario?"

"What are the learning opportunities I can find in this scenario?"

"How might this experience benefit me in the long term?"

"What skills might I develop from overcoming this challenge?"

"What unique advantage might I have over my competitors who haven't overcome a similar challenge?"

Since these questions aim to force you to think critically and break free from your initial response, they should be difficult and open-ended.

Recognizing your inclinations and formulating questions that go against them is critical. We can achieve this by making ourselves think like someone who reacts differently. Consider asking yourself, "What would a completely calm person do in this scenario?" if you are anxious. Make an image of this hypothetical other person and force yourself to describe their thoughts, feelings, and behaviors. By doing this, your brain will be subtly primed to react in a way that is significantly more consistent with the results you want.

Persuasion Tips for Everyday Use

The capacity to convince is a vital quality for any entrepreneur. Often, we have a wonderful idea, but we may have problems selling it to an investor. Meanwhile, we see other people with not-so-innovative initiatives who can make deals and gain financial support. Do you wonder why? How we sell our ideas is critical.

Persuasion is important for those who want to undertake their own business venture and those who work in the corporate world because it is a characteristic that can lead the professional ahead in the company and, consequently, in their career. When dealing with bosses and colleagues, the power to influence is beneficial in situations of discord and when presenting new work proposals in the company. Even to discuss wages and benefits, one needs to be persuasive.

In the book Maximum Influence by Kurt W. Mortensen, the author lists 12 laws he considers universal for effective persuasion. Here, we list five of them to familiarize yourself with and gradually learn to master. Knowing these laws can be used or avoided when necessary. Let's take a look at them:

1- Law of Connectivity

Developing a rapport with the other person is the first step towards natural persuasion. "The law of connectivity says that the more someone feels connected or similar to you, and loved or attracted to you, the more persuasive you become," Mortensen writes in his book. This relationship does not have to be long-standing; it can be established immediately through casual talk.

Whether before a presentation, in a brief discussion, over the phone, or in another context, it is important to always attempt to come across as sincere as possible. You cannot come across as forced or phony. Simply speaking, be kind, and use humor and natural body language. The four essential components of connectedness are comprehension, empathy, resemblance, and attraction. Your grin, face, and body language contribute to your perceived attractiveness and appeal. Being empathetic is another effective technique to establish a connection with someone since it demonstrates your similarity to them.

2. Expectation Law

What does the term "self-actualizing" prophecy mean? It's where you picture yourself in a particular light, and that envisioning brings that image to pass. An experiment where students take a test after being informed they are the best at a particular subject is an example of this. The identical test was administered to other pupils in secret. Interestingly, despite being selected at random, the students who received the compliment did better.

Understanding this can help you manipulate events to your desired outcome. "The law of expectation uses expectations to influence reality and create results," Mortensen states. This indicates that people typically behave as expected, which can be useful when influencing someone to act or believe a particular way.

There are several methods to convey your expectations of someone, including through word choice, body language, and voice intonation. The idea is to organize your words and body language to make the person you are attempting to convince want or need to respond in the way you anticipate.

3. The Contrast Law

"The law of contrast explains how we are affected when someone offers us two different options, and in sequence," adds Mortensen. You most likely won't want to shell out several thousand dollars for repairs if a mechanic examines your vehicle and determines that the brakes, battery, and gearbox must be changed. It doesn't seem so horrible to spend a few hundred bucks when you return to the garage, and he tells you that the brakes are all that need to be changed.

The law of contrast is this. Understanding this law means opposing value and price. There is always a second. By contrasting the two options, we can skew or broaden the perception of price, effort, or time in the eyes of investors, bosses, and customers. You can persuade someone to select your chosen option by employing this strategy.

4. The Scarcity Law

We often complete purchases more quickly if we believe the product is restricted. Events of this magnitude, such as Black Friday, are one example. Because the deal is time-limited and there are limited quantities, customers in the US form lines before the stores open.

One of the most effective ways to persuade someone to accept you offer to instill a sense of urgency in them, the consumer or target audience. According to the rule of scarcity, an item's value rises with its decreasing thickness. People behave more rapidly out of fear of missing out on a good chance; this is a crucial concept in the persuasive process. Scarcity is not necessary to persuade someone. It suffices that you conjure up this picture.

Law of Esteem No. 5

People require a great deal of approval and gratitude. When attempting to convince someone, considering this can help. However, the author does not discuss lying. Seeking genuine praise for others has significantly more impact. Therefore, it is preferable to identify positive qualities in the individual or business rather than creating praiseworthy features. It is always preferable to congratulate someone on something modest and honest than to attempt to discredit him for a significant reason.

According to Mortensen, you should make it a habit to compliment others daily and strive to make them feel truly significant.

Marketing and Deception

You've undoubtedly heard the adage "You can sell anything if you have the right mind" regarding company sales.

To sell a product to a consumer, one must know the salesperson's persuasive strategies. Used car salespeople have a reputation for taking any subpar vehicle and making it seem much better than it is. This is for good reason.

Despite this behavior, they are nearly invariably criticized for their use of manipulation. It might be difficult to distinguish between manipulation and persuasion. Particularly in an industry with significant financial risks and employment opportunities at risk, this boundary may be crossed so frequently that it becomes difficult to distinguish between the two. In this chapter, we'll explain how salespeople utilize manipulation to effectively market their goods, along with how you might use the same strategies in your own endeavors or business.

Before ever launching a product, businesses must always meet the wants of their customers. The salesman will convince—or, in this case, manipulate—you into purchasing the product once it has been designed with that in mind. As a result, many things are made to appeal to our primal emotional needs. Making money is the primary motivation behind most salesperson's strategies, essentially "lite" or recycled forms of earlier manipulation. Keeping these points in mind, let us discuss how these strategies operate. Presenting the client with data or figures is one way. A salesperson is attempting to upsell $75 bike helmets. He mentions to the next customer he sees that children between the ages of six and fourteen are more likely to be involved in deadly bike accidents in the past year. He finds it easier because it relates to the customer's empathy. By appealing to the customers' natural desire to shield their kids from harm and ensure they don't suffer injuries. The salesman will go one step further and offer the consumer a one-time deal with a 15% discount if he buys it immediately. Little to no time is left for decision-making due to this manipulation. Furthermore, the salesman frequently offers this alleged 15% discount to every possible client. giving the impression that his sale is exclusive to them alone. Customers are under pressure to buy the helmet immediately since they believe it would be irrefutable and nearly impossible to do otherwise. In persuading the buyer that this offer is unethical to reject, it also capitalizes on the human desire for exclusivity. If the buyer believes they are the only ones receiving this great price on the bike helmet, automobile, or other item, they will accept it. The salesperson has ultimately sold something at an extremely marked-up price when, in truth, its value is significantly less than what it is being marketed for due to these sales practices. It should be understood that they take this action to bolster your confidence in the transaction. Recall that their goal is to profit while meeting the consumer's needs. Sales and manipulation are fundamentally psychologically driven. If you've ever watched any advertising, you probably noticed that the people utilizing the products appear happy or as though their lives have been completed just by using them. Professional businesses take great care to avoid doing anything that may give them a bad or tarnished reputation because of the manipulation used in sales. As a result, they typically take pride in producing high-quality products. In light of this, how precisely can you steer clear of deceptive sales techniques? The solution to that issue is similar to avoiding other manipulation techniques, but the result differs. You must keep your opinions to yourself, so let's say, for example, that you have done your homework and know that a particular car may be worth $25,000. When you visit a car dealership, the salesperson tries to upsell you on the vehicle by adding many unnecessary luxury items. You should tell the salesperson, "Hey buddy, I know I can get this junk for 25k somewhere else," directly and assertively. To put it plainly, most auto salespeople take a chance on the possibility that customers may be wary and decide not to defend themselves. Therefore, when making any purchases, act bravely and with assurance. Being aggressive and self-assured conveys to the seller that you take business seriously and might be hard to fool, if not impossible. Finally, Let me briefly explain how advertising manipulates your emotions to persuade you to buy its goods. One of the key strategies used by advertising agencies is what psychologists refer to as the "Fear of Missing Out." This implies that if Apple produces a new iPhone and runs many adverts for it, they are essentially betting more on cultural phenomena than on the advertisements selling the phone. In other words, if everyone you know and everyone in your immediate vicinity starts purchasing iPhones, you will be highly tempted to do the same. Most of your reasoning will come from your subconscious, such as wanting to fit in and avoid being left out of the latest developments. Ad firms also prefer to utilize sexual tactics. As everyone has heard, "sex sells." This is evident in many subtle ways that products are marketed and the forms they may take. These characteristics have made it such that you should always pay great attention to advertisements you see to determine whether they are trying to appeal to your intrinsic or subconscious inclinations. This contains elements like women wearing skimpy clothing and seductive shapes and figures in the advertisement. You can better resist advertising now that you know how it affects basic emotions. When making a significant purchase, the most crucial thing to remember is to ignore any feelings you may have and instead deal only with facts and logic. It may or may not surprise you that emotion, not reason, drives most motivation for a goal. Because of this preference for emotion over reason, most deceptive sales techniques, if not all, aim to appeal to our feelings rather than reason. When attending anything, keep this in mind and disregard the emotional indicators. This might be challenging, particularly if you're buying a home. Realtors may employ various real estate industry strategies to persuade you to purchase a home. Their primary ploy will be to persuade you of something unimportant—the emotional attraction of a house's beauty. You can always refute a realtor's emotional assertions.

What NLP Is For

Natural Language Processing (NLP) can prove highly advantageous in some domains where individuals strive for enhancement and exceptional performance. Given our shared existence and common challenges, the problems that arise are frequently similar for many individuals.

Stress management is an area where NLP has demonstrated significant value. The negative ramifications of stress have been extensively examined over the past few decades, and we now understand that it can result in many health concerns. By employing Natural Language Processing (NLP) techniques, one might attain a more optimistic perspective on life and significantly reduce daily stress levels.

There will be a notable enhancement in your relationships. As your communication skills improve and you become adept at actively listening and comprehending the messages of others, you will certainly witness the growth of your interpersonal relationships.

Attaining excellence and fostering personal growth are essential objectives of NLP . Through its teachings, you will progressively acquire the skills to harness your complete capabilities effectively throughout various aspects of your life. Even if you cannot achieve exceptional performance in every endeavor (which is likely unattainable), you will experience contentment with yourself and the exertions you invest. The experience of contentment will also impact your outcomes, leading to notable enhancements.

Adopting NLP in your life will lead to improved time management, significant lifestyle modifications, and genuine gratitude. Although human beings are inherently flawed, striving for greatness whenever feasible is nonetheless important. You will enhance your self-awareness by cultivating these abilities and mindsets and ultimately confronting your apprehensions. Engaging in this activity will develop a greater sense of self-appreciation.

Neuro-Linguistic Programming in Therapy

NLP therapists consult with clients to assess their cognitive and behavioral patterns, psychological well-being, and objectives. The trainer will motivate individuals to uncover and enhance their strengths by analyzing their profiles and empowering them to develop alternative strategies to replace unproductive ones. The technique will facilitate individuals in attaining significant milestones in their rehabilitation within the counseling framework.

Advocates of NLP assert that this approach offers rapid and long-lasting outcomes, enhancing understanding of behavioral and cognitive patterns. NLP often facilitates the establishment of a meaningful dialogue between conscious and subconscious brain systems, thereby assisting individuals in enhancing their imaginative and problem-solving capacities. Several advocates of NLP compare the approach to CBT and contend that NLP could yield substantial outcomes in a shorter duration.

Neuro-Linguistic Programming has been employed since its inception to tackle various issues. Comprising:

Communication problems

Attention deficit hyperactivity disorder (ADHD)

Emotions of fear, anxiety, and phobia

Experiencing post-traumatic stress disorder

Schizophrenia

Depression

Personality on the brink of instability

Dependency

Fixations and irresistible urges

Anticipating and preparing for future events or outcomes.

This method, referred to as future pacing, necessitates the practitioner to assist the client to see their approach to accomplishing a task in the future. The NLP practitioner will observe the client's responses while they engage in this activity.

Future pacing aims to ascertain the efficacy of a change in progress. The practitioner will ascertain this determination by analyzing the subject's nonverbal cues. If the client's body language remains unchanged from earlier attempts, the intervention was completely unsuccessful. Another objective of future pacing is to establish a favorable transformation for the future. The customer must adopt a more effective strategy when faced with an issue, particularly when the potential consequences are harmful.

An important advantage of employing future pacing is that it allows the client to gain familiarity with a specific scenario before their involvement. They will already have a prearranged favorable response prepared. Future pace, while dependent on visualization, is based on the assumption that the mind cannot distinguish between a vividly visualized scenario and an actual one. Although it may initially seem peculiar, it is extremely effortless to manipulate your mind into perceiving things favorably.

The theory of future pacing centers on the notion that when you mentally see something positively, your topic becomes an exemplary behavior model. Even a hypothetical initial encounter serves as a valuable point of reference. Essentially, your actions acknowledge and embrace the initial mental image despite its lack of authenticity. Your brain unconsciously generates the desired alteration you wish to undergo when you face the stimulus again in the future—this time, in actuality. Fundamentally, it operates on the principle that repeated practice leads to perfection.

The sound of something moving swiftly through the air.

This Natural Language Processing (NLP) method aims to redirect cognitive patterns to eliminate undesired behaviors and promote desirable ones. Your subconscious mind usually prompts you to behave in a manner that it considers most suitable. The goodness of the activity hinges on several distinct factors. The customer is advised to adopt new constructive habits instead of succumbing to negative ones.

Swishing typically necessitates the utilization of visual clues and auditory stimuli. The visualizations are accompanied by acoustic effects to promote the transition from bad to good behaviors, discouraging undesirable behavior.

In essence, swishing is advantageous for several reasons. It can alleviate emotions such as humiliation and stress for several individuals. Indeed, acquiring the skill of swishing can effectively resolve distressing circumstances. Naturally, this strategy is most effective when employed to address minor problems rather than substantial ones.

Utilising Internal Representations To Captivate People's Imagination

Have you ever considered what goes through someone's mind when communicating with them? Our unconscious mind interprets everything stated to us internally, allowing us to understand the meaning of a statement. You might visualize the large fox and the bushes internally when you read the line, "Sarah saw a big fox behind the bushes."

Now, note how the next two sentences differ from each other:

"Comprehensing psychology is challenging."

Comprehending psychology is a challenging task.

The two statements have the same logical meaning, but each has a distinct internal representation. Several NLP patterns make use of this concept.

You can use terms and phrases like "consider," "imagine," "suppose," "think about," and so on to guide someone else's imagination with this concept.

When you use such terms, you are effectively giving your topic instructions. These words have a subtle persuading effect when they are uttered. Nothing the subject can do but decline to listen to you.

Words like "imagine," "consider," and so on create mental images that encourage you to do just that. As a result, you are persuaded without meaning to be.

Validation of Internal Representations

L. Michael Hall and RintuBasu have written about internal representations in their books.

Bostrom and Thomas (1983) discussed internal world representations and their importance for communication. Developing a thorough understanding of internal representations can aid in communicating effectively.

In his publication from 2012, B. Lewis went into further detail regarding internal representations and their importance in persuasion.

A Brief Narrative

Brenda, my coworker, is a mother of two. Brenda's remarks about her kids naturally jumped into our discussion about internal images.

Being a parent is challenging; thus, having a solid understanding of NLP persuasive techniques is quite beneficial. Brenda explained how she used the ideas of internal representations to influence her daughter.

Her daughter insisted on going to the beach in a long, frilly white dress. Brenda persuaded her to switch to a bathing suit by imagining her gorgeous dress stained in mud, ripped at some spots by the pebbles, and with the frills falling off. Consider the possibility that you will never be able to wear it somewhere else.

Almost immediately, her daughter consented to wear the bathing suit instead. Take note of Brenda's use of vivid imagery. She might have simply said, "Your dress will be ruined," but she could get what she wanted by using more detail.

Why It's Important to Understand Internal Representations

Mental images are crucial. Once you understand how people visualize things in their minds, you can easily modify your language to achieve your desired results.

The mental representation principle can be used for any type of terrible news. For example, you may say, "Your skillset would be more useful elsewhere; we have to let you go," rather than, "You are fired because you are incompetent."

While these statements convey the same idea, their internal representations differ.

The First Things You Should Know About Internal Representations

The following are some essential details regarding internal representations:

When you want your target to think a certain way, use internal representations to subtly offer them a direct order. For instance, "How about we begin a dream journal daily?"

You may truly elicit specific scenarios from your subjects by employing specific language.

Inquiries can also guide imagination, which means that they can also be used to influence internal images.

Language Hypnotic Techniques

We've covered the mentality required to comprehend the usage of hypnotic language and the core idea that persuasion relies on. Let's now discuss the actual persuasive strategies you should study and use.

1. Setting the stage

I couldn't figure out why, but Elton John's hit song "Philadelphia Freedom" would not stop playing in my head for months. After learning about the priming process, I realized what the song was doing to me.

The priming technique is based on the assumption that concepts and ideas can be ingrained into the mind without the subject's knowledge. Let's take a closer look at this method.

What Does Priming Entail?

When a stimulus affects your reactions long after it has been exposed to you, it is referred to as priming. Allow me to illustrate this with an example.

When asked to come up with a word that rhymes with "log" after being given a list of words that include the words "pet," "cat," and "wolf," your most likely response will be "dog." When you hear the word "wolf," you'll probably think of a dog because the term "cat" typically pairs with "dog," and since dogs are pets and rhyme with "log," you'll probably answer "dog."

You can see that your mind chose the word "dog" from that shortlist. This is the process of priming. It causes an influence on your subconscious that often lasts one or two days, although occasionally, it might last longer.

Knowing this approach can help you develop a keen sense of self-observation. If you truly observe, you will find that most of our decisions are made subconsciously. Have you ever realized that your buddy had just told you she was feeling blue, and you were wondering why it felt natural to wear that blue blouse today? Have you ever wondered why you wanted spaghetti for dinner on your way home from work, only to realize later that you had caught a glimpse of an Italian travel billboard? If you truly pay attention, you will find that your subconscious mind's response to specific signals has predetermined many of your actions.

How can you do it if you are not conscious that you are doing this? The idea is simple: whenever you decide on anything seemingly random, like what music to listen to while driving, pause and ask yourself: Is there something I'm picking up on subconsciously influencing my decision?

Subconscious priming aims to influence your word choice by tricking your subconscious. Long after you instill certain words in your memory, you choose to use them.

Priming brings related ideas and thoughts to your attention, which helps you remember words but also generates new ideas, concepts, memories, and thoughts.

In essence, this method either opens your mind to fresh information or reintroduces previously held beliefs that are readily accessible and lurk beneath the surface of your subconscious. When you get a new car, for example, you begin to notice other cars that are comparable to yours.

Different Kinds of Priming

These are the various forms of priming.

Conceptual priming: When related thoughts prime a response, this happens. For example, "hat" could be a prime word for "head."

Semantic priming is the process by which one meaning shapes subsequent ideas. Conceptual priming is comparable to it.

Semantic priming is a strategy used to describe two or more related concepts where it is improbable that thinking about one will lead to thinking about the other. For example, you won't think of Venus if someone says the word "sun" to you. This method is handy when you don't want someone to think of a certain thought or recall certain details.

Associative Priming: Associative priming is the process of priming a particular related notion. For example, the word "bread" primes the word "butter."

Repetitive priming is frequently repeating a word or idea to sway your subsequent thoughts. For example, you can be inspired to follow your interest later on if you listen to a song about it again.

Let's examine priming's goals, objectives, and advantages in the context of persuasion.

The Primary and Fundamental Ideas of NLP

We covered the three parts of NLP in the earlier chapters. The three main elements and ideas that influence NLP will be covered in more detail in this section.

Subjectivity

Any person can have subjective representations based on their experiences. The five senses and language are utilized to form the representation, according to Bandler and Grinder. The subjectivities of auditory, smell, taste, and vision comprise the conventional senses of the subjective conscious experience. An excellent illustration of this is when we have something "on our minds" and then imagine what "we see," "what we hear," and "what we taste" will happen. After that, "what we feel," "what we smell," and eventually "what we think" will come into play. Subjective representations shape, form, and influence an individual. Currently, NLP is regarded as the study applied to every subjective experience.

Subjective, sense-based representations identify and describe a person's actions. It might be verbal or nonverbal, incompetent, or regarded as a sick behavior that undermines all skillful habits equally. The representations of the senses have the power to affect or modify behaviors.

Being Aware

This occurs when a person's concept shifts from conscious to conscious and unconscious. Subjective representations occur on the level of that person's awareness and are known as the unconscious mind.

Acquiring knowledge

Modeling is another name for it, and it is a learning strategy based on imitation. It's well recognized that it can facilitate experience in any kind of activity. Understanding and articulating the description of the activities involved is crucial. And be aware of the experience's consequences.

The Foundations of Nonverbal Learning

NLP has four well-known pillars or foundations, which are as follows: rapport

Anyone can develop and sustain positive relationships with those around them with the help of NLP . This is the capacity to swiftly get to know someone and establish a connection. When there is understanding, trust can be easily established and will aid in building relationships with people through being aware of other people's inclinations, forecasts, and plans.

Recognizing the Sensory

The primary means of achieving this is through social interaction. For example, accepting an invitation to someone else's home. You'll first notice the colors they've chosen, the décor, the fragrance, and any nearby noises. The majority of this differs from what you have at home. When you utilize neuro-linguistic programming or NLP , you'll discover that everything around you seems richer because you're paying closer attention and using all your senses.

Result-Oriented Thinking

The result is always referred to or called the aim when you perform something. They facilitate making connections with an individual's goals or preferences. This is good for the mind and soul and helps prevent thinking about anything bad that might happen. Making important and wise decisions is made easier using this method.

Adaptability in an Individual's Conduct

This indicates that an individual can perform a task more comfortably than they are accustomed to. This occurs when your routine and method are not sensible or adaptable. Being adaptable is essential for success while using NLP. NLP aids in gaining fresh viewpoints and developing constructive behaviors.

Why is it necessary for someone to learn NLP?

NLP's advantages and applications have been discussed. We must clarify why you should become knowledgeable about NLP. For several reasons, such as: • One develops into a strong and excellent communicator.

• The ability to recognize nonverbal cues improves.

• Boost sensory awareness and the subconscious mind.

• Empowerment has a purpose.

• Diminish phobias and anxieties.

• Capable of emotional regulation and sound thought.

- Grow in friendships and relationships, both personally and professionally.
- There is an increase in achievement and success rate.
- Give up bad habits and develop positive self-talk.
- Possessing the ability to constructively acquire information from others.
- Use effective and efficient communication.

The NLP Training Levels

After realizing the significance of NLP training, it's critical to understand the steps necessary for success. Numerous establishments are recognized for their ability to plan, manage, and provide these kinds of programs. When pursuing a course, enrolling in just one institution is best. Three stages comprise NLP training:

NLP Expert

This is regarded as the beginning level of NLP instruction; anyone can enroll, regardless of experience requirements. It entails studying the fundamentals of NLP , as well as the applied methods and components. They are considered when using all of grace and competence. They consider all the necessary methods and abilities to effectively carry out their responsibilities while making sure that it will positively impact their life. The topics of the study are how to handle problems in families, enterprises, and relationships. Additionally, it is simpler to experience positive personal progress in schooling when one learns all the tactics. The course covers the theory of practical use of NLP skills. It promotes increased confidence and the elimination of phobias and dread.

Master NLP

This second phase increases the amount of content to be learned, along with more specifics, intricate data, and models to apply. It is more intricate and uses more vocabulary and modeling. They ultimately acquire abilities that will alter their ideals and outlook on life. The capacity for empathy and the ability to get along better with friends, family, and coworkers.

People who reach this level will have updated communication features and approaches. They consist mostly of quantum linguistics, retraining, and discovery. It includes understanding individual values, the capacity for unconscious behavior, and the reasons behind and methods of diverse thought patterns.

Their personality, advanced techniques, and submodalities under advanced NLP are also covered in the course. Mediation skills, as well as any sophisticated language negotiation skills. The scheduled training occurs in many locations and helps alter relationships, health, and business. And eventually contributes to the growth of a happy existence.

As a result, the individual who possesses the dark triad of personality traits is halfway between having a pleasant disposition and showing symptoms of a mental illness. The line is fairly thin, as far as we can see. Strictly speaking, to determine with certainty whether an individual has a psychological diagnosis—a dark triad of personality—it is required to seek further consultation with a psychiatrist in addition to a psychologist. Psychodiagnostic techniques must also be used. In addition, because the carriers of psychological traits—narcissism, psychopathy, and Machiavellianism—are very intelligent in their behavior of psychological guidance from immediately obvious, a hypothetical diagnosis—a dark triad of personality—is stated simply and rapidly. However, rigorous psychodiagnosis should be used in the future to support or contradict this theory. Unless the psychologist wishes to take responsibility for his remarks and not just present a cunning, enigmatic front during the interview.

It is inappropriate to define psychopathy, narcissism, and Machiavellianism in the same article. Each of their three dark triad personality traits merits a lengthy, independent publication. We will now describe these events in generic terms. This will be sufficient to comprehend the dark triad's main ideas.

What Does a Psychologist Understand About Narcissism?

A personality trait known as narcissism occurs when an individual exhibits overtly inflated self-esteem and visible insufficient narcissism, all the while ignoring the needs and psychological reactions of others. Intriguingly, narcissism may be a psychologically protective or compensatory response to the opposite and meticulously hidden traits—anxiety, excessive neuroticism, and low self-esteem—that the "narcissist" may be hiding from the outside world. Thus, the subject of narcissism's beginnings is never easy to answer.

At the turn of the 19th and 20th centuries, the earliest psychoanalysts introduced the notion of narcissism into psychology. The name derives from its connections to the Greek myth of the lovely young man Narcissus, who turned down the Nymph Echo's love proposal instead of gazing at his exquisite reflection in the stream. The gods drove the lovely young man into madness as a punishment for his ridiculous narcissism, unbridled self-centeredness, and contempt for the real feelings of others. First, he fell in love with his reflection in the stream—that is, how one can fall in love with a woman—and then they transformed him into a flower known as a narcissist.

Narcissism can take two extreme forms (and everything in between) depending on the degree of narcissistic traits, an individual's age, and his past experiences.

1. The version of the norm takes the shape of a subtle accent that highlights each person's

uniqueness in the human mind. According to certain psychologists, women in particular, this somewhat enhanced level of narcissism is psychologically normal at specific stages of sexuality and personality development. Some psychologists claim that women with moderate levels of narcissism are more adaptive in how they organize their social and personal lives as well as how to create and maintain their outward appearance.

This most likely includes addressing the psychologists who contend that self-love is essential. In particular, psychological counseling is a major field for this topic. Women who exhibit low self-esteem, high levels of neuroticism, dependence on a spouse, and a willingness to compromise their objectives for the sake of relationships are often the targets of psychotherapy. Indeed, there is a reasonable edge to this, if only to highlight how ridiculous the concept of narcissism is.

2. A type of personality disorder where people exhibit abnormally strong and insufficient narcissistic traits in their interactions with reality. Such a person frequently harbors exaggerated beliefs about his sexual orientation, physical attributes, and accomplishments. He is consumed by illusions about his accomplishments, the expectation of an unwaveringly positive attitude, and unquestioned devotion from others, seeking validation for his specialness and importance. A person like that loses their capacity for empathy. He has a strong desire to be free from all restrictions and disregards the needs of others. He attributes his shortcomings to the cunning and jealousy of his critics.

A personal case of narcissism occurs when sexual attraction is added to all of the above but to one's body rather than other people. This is similar to sexual deviation in narcissism. As a result, in this instance, autophilia, or autosexuality, the narcissistic disorder is typically categorized as a mental illness. Since scatophilia is generally not linked to the dark triad of personality traits, we won't discuss it. In summary, narcissism manifested as autophilia calls for a course of psychological assistance in the form of psychotherapy, assuming, of course, that the individual needs and desires it. Consultation with a psychologist and/or psychiatrist is necessary. Thankfully, our nation has very few punitive practices in psychology and psychiatry.

The psychologist can use the questionnaire to evaluate non-clinical narcissism, or narcissism as a personality trait, to determine the client's level of narcissism and its presence. The NPI, or Narcissistic Personality Inventory. The psychologist could suggest speaking with a psychiatrist to provide additional clarity in clinical instances.

Commercial Sense

Nothing screams "professional" quite like a stellar CV, career growth and promotion opportunities, inspiring leadership, positive staff relations, and reasonable overhead. Our work lives play a significant role in what so many of us value:

They allow us to put food on the table, pay the mortgage, and send the kids to school.

They allow us to enjoy the occasional holiday break.

They help many people see their value.

Our career performance greatly influences our overall well-being. Our feeling of purpose in working to support ourselves financially and further our professional aspirations shapes our identities, self-perceptions, and interactions with the corporate world.

Too many of us battle to grow in our careers and be happy with what we do. With little success, some of us make a lot of effort to climb the ladder. Some of us have no trouble moving up the ladder, but our jobs become unpleasant because we don't get along with our coworkers. To the great cost of our happiness, many among us work at a job that we know isn't aligned with who we are or what we want. Some of us opt to stick with the safety of our well-paying jobs rather than taking the risk of pursuing something better in our careers. What if you knew how to design the work-life balance you desire? What would it feel like to have the career success you desire at the organization you want to work for, at the salary you want, and with the kind of rewarding and interesting coworkers that support your professional development?

The secret to all of that and more is NLP .Neuro-linguistic programming is a widely used method by organizations, employers, and management teams to train their entire workforce. Why? Because it creates improved output and efficiency, more time to concentrate on outcomes rather than issues, happier, more driven employees, higher customer satisfaction, and a stronger bottom line. NLP is just about learning how to think and express yourself to construct your life experience; no special magic is involved. It demonstrates that you can alter your feelings about where you are by becoming aware of how you think and how to adjust things that don't work.

Even though you might not be seeking NLP for assistance in the corporate world, once you begin to grasp the principles and acquire the tools, these practices become applicable in all facets of your life. Ultimately, it's about your overall experience, not just your professional one. However, NLP 's effects will significantly improve the performance of your business or work, making it feel less stressful, less productive, and devoid of the need to aim higher.

Consciousness

Without the advantage of consciousness, what good is all of this? One main goal reached by all of these ideas in this book is self-awareness. The goal of NLP is not limited to helping you get on the correct track for weight loss and exercise; it also extends beyond enhancing your relationships and professional performance. Being self-aware is the only way to achieve any of these objectives. How much of your life is spent going through the motions and scheming according to your established routine? How often do you divert your attention from the feelings and experiences you are having at any one time? We are not meant to be mindless machines that obey commands, carry out mental computer programs, uphold the status quo, and carry on with childhood beliefs.

Our purpose is to grow, learn, and live our lives. Our goal in being here is to build on the knowledge and expertise we have already gained. The only way to accomplish this is by awareness.

Being self-aware allows you to learn from your experiences and yourself. It also helps you recognize what drives your behavior in different contexts, which boosts your confidence because you are no longer doubting your motivations or identity. Instead, you are just trying to understand them. Awareness of what is no longer effective in your life might help you recognize it; when you understand what needs to change—awareness—you may accept how to change. In essence, what you are learning with neuro-linguistic programming is awareness. Putting your core values and beliefs into perspective, along with how you came to hold them and if they still apply to your current situation, transforms how you view every event in life.

The next step is to identify a need, which should be quite clear. You learned all the details about your prospect in Step 2. This is the ideal moment to determine if you can assist them with their particular issue or difficulty. Although it may seem apparent, many salespeople skip this phase and go straight to the close. This is a particularly crucial stage. Surprisingly, you are searching for "No's." As strange as it may seem, a "No" is always preferable to a "Maybe."

This book contains Frank's account of how he first overspent time pursuing prospects who said, "Maybe," or "Follow up with me next week." After doing some calculations, he realized that his chances of closing the prospect decreased significantly if he failed to close them on the first attempt. He estimated that, in actuality, seventy percent of his transactions were closed on the first try. On the second, only 23% were closed. The closure rate for the third follow-up was a mere 7%. Frank discovered that he sold significantly more if he invested more time chatting with potential customers. Are you running after those who said, "Maybe?" for the better part of the day?

Okay, give up! The sea is full of fish now. Your chances of closing one are significantly higher.

So, how do you assess whether your good or service is necessary? As expected, the method is straightforward. This method is called a soft or test closure by some and a conditional close by others. "Do you see any value to this?" is your inquiry. or "Is it fair to say that if we solved this problem for you, then this would be valuable to you?" Alternatively, using our automobile analogy again, "Would you be ready to buy if we could get this for you in blue?" You can figure out a few more, I'm sure.

The goal is to determine whether or not the prospect is serious. Right now, we merely want to know if the person thinks of themselves as a potential client; objections are not a concern. Eighty percent of a salesperson's time is usually spent with non-buying customers. This was a mistake I used to do. I had to switch employment every few months because of this. I had to constantly close at first since I would need to bring in many new clients. After some time, following up with the prospects who responded "maybe" took up most of my time. Give up torturing yourself. Remove these individuals. Get rid of those leading you on and spend time with those interested in purchasing. My lesson was learned. Also, consider how much more assured you'll feel knowing that you'll interact with potential customers 80% of the time. Selling will be simpler the more confident you are.

Benefits of Natural Language Processing

Benefits are the potential positive outcomes of NLP in this instance. What are the benefits of applying NLP , then? First of all, it facilitates transformation and the adoption of novel concepts. This facilitates integrating new experiences into an individual's life. Any victim of hardship must acquire new skills and modify certain characteristics to overcome their issues. Thus, it is beneficial to implement change and the adoption of new ideas in daily life.

When a person is aware of their environment and at the moment, NLP can be applied. This aids in maintaining control over one's current relationships. This is essentially accomplished by comprehending a specific individual's mental, physical, and psychological characteristics. These methods aid in comprehending and resolving any issue, no matter how minor or large. Everything keeps the person aware and on their toes, making them approachable and comfortable. This benefit applies to both men and women and is useful in daily life. It is a simple method of accessing a live, breathing human conversation.

It also assists people in resolving difficult issues related to their relationships. To make this happen, one must have access to the person's darkest, most mysterious thoughts and emotions. Because of this, the NLP is appropriate for the task above. Since NLP reads the mind, it is easy to integrate it with therapy, which addresses psychological feelings, to achieve the aim the professional is pursuing. Several perspectives on interpersonal interactions will be examined, leading to an excellent solution. This means moving ahead and standing without turning around when utilized at last.

Ultimately, getting rid of some beliefs that prevent someone from growing up is beneficial. The sufferer gains confidence and learns to lead a regular life with the help of treatment and the specialist's ongoing supervision. One of the objectives of the therapy is this. The entire process of recovery and redemption is significant and wise in every way. Without NLP, a person is more susceptible to negative and destructive concepts. NLP is a valuable ally and resource in this field, and the experts who see it through are as vital.

Does NLP Have a Negative Side?

NLP has many benefits, but it is not without flaws. It is not flawless, just like everything else in the world. The first drawback is that the focus is mostly on the patient rather than the patient and the therapist together. The therapist must speak with the patient to comprehend their issues. If the patient is unwilling to share personal information with the therapist, this may be ineffective and ultimately lead to an unresolved problem. Therapy's goal is to treat; in this instance, that is impossible. Another drawback is that both partners must put in a lot of work. For NLP to be effective, both parties must put in their best and most efficient effort; they cannot simply wait for miracles to happen. While the client must be willing to open up to the therapist, the therapist must comprehend the client's issues. By using this therapeutic approach, it is ensured that both parties are making more and bigger developments. Often, when one of the parties falters, the others follow suit and fail collectively to complete the work at hand. Lastly, the session needs to be prepared for.

This is simply anticipating actions, words, or even questions. The entire process will fail if this is ignored. It indicates that the therapy is ineffective and a waste of time. This merely serves to highlight how seriously NLP takes its seriousness. This is to prevent mayhem.

What are the Main Strategies for NLP Improvement?

There are other techniques to enhance NLP, but I'll only touch on a few here to provide a concise summary. Understanding the NLP language can help one become more proficient in the field. Once one is fluent in the language, carrying out the therapy the clients require will be simple. Additionally, one can enhance NLP by refining their coded NLP language. NLP has a coded language of its own. As I previously stated, NLP can be better comprehended by seeing someone's brain waves and activity. Once one comprehends how they function, NLP will only become more advanced. Understanding the issue at hand is another method. Put simply, this indicates that problem-solving will be straightforward and quick once one can recognize and comprehend it.

Managing The Suffering Caused By Strained Relationships

Most people probably feel sadness or sorrow when a meaningful relationship ends. It is not shocking that living without mutual experiences creates a void in our lives that takes some getting used to, and loneliness is a typical occurrence.

Some folks, though, are heartbroken. When loved ones leave them for someone else, they feel betrayed, disgraced, and rejected. These emotions, combined with the fear of being alone, the loss of love, and the sensation of being let down, can easily turn into self-pity, uncontrollable rage, and melancholy.

The reliance that comes with "being in love" with someone or something is the cause of the strong emotional emotions.

I frequently tell my clients that I know men who are steamtrain enthusiasts "in love." For a desired postage stamp, some people have even killed.

These emotions are a result of programs that are encoded similarly to other programs.

Naturally, I missed my daughter when she moved out of the house, but my main concern was her safety. I sent her my best wishes. I was not depressed. Not in love, but that is love.

As this book's introduction explains, I begin my treatment with clients suffering from the heartbreak of a broken relationship by educating them about brain programming codes.

Next, I ask them to consider a person they see frequently but don't care much for. A TV news anchor is a popular option. I could pick someone they knew in the past but hardly ever saw. The TV host does, however, leave the prospect that the client may run into their ex-partner by chance.

Then, I ask them to consider the person they are mourning while also considering the television host. I persuade them to shift their partner's (let's call him Fred Nerk) image until it EXACTLY obscures and aligns with the TV personality (let's call him Barry Basket). I want them to fade in Barry, then fade out Barry, then fade in Fred. I ask them to repeat the procedure as fast as possible, calling out "Barry Basket" and "Fred Nerk" when the images appear.

I ask them to repeat the activity for the next seven nights before they go to bed. Usually, that is sufficient to relieve them of the worst emotions, but only if they take action.

An illustration of this in action.

An elderly woman in her thirties visited me; her husband accompanied her. He intended to part ways with her and their kids. She couldn't stop crying.

I questioned if he truly wanted to part ways with her. "Yes," he said.

When she decided she no longer wanted him, I asked whether he felt he could handle it. He responded, "Yes," as she stopped crying. I walked her through the outlined procedure while asking him to wait outside.

I performed some hypnosis on her the next week to help her feel more confident.

I believed that our third visit was to charge her husband for my services and inconvenience and annoy him over a fifty-mile trip. "I wish he would just clear off now," she remarked.

As an illustration

A fifty-year-old man had been dating for a few years. His girlfriend left my client after she "fell in love" with a man she worked with. He had been unhappy and anxious for several months and required time off work. "Go see Harold," advised his general practitioner.

After going through the procedure I've outlined with him, he improved significantly within a week. But when he saw her drive by his house, and she grinned at him, he claimed to have become "upset."

When Would I Require Someone to Be Manipulated?

You may find yourself wanting to control someone else fairly frequently. One instance is the desire to close a deal with a salesperson. By employing some of the manipulation techniques we will discuss, the salesman can provide the necessary opportunities to build rapport swiftly and effortlessly. They will discover that the sale with the victim—or, in this case, the customer—will close swiftly once they have established that rapport.

When you can convince someone to take the time to listen to your offer, they are far less likely to say no to you. This can also apply to offering advice when necessary, asking for assistance, and any other situation you're attempting to get your way. The notion is that you can use manipulation to get what you want if you want to persuade someone else to agree with you and ensure that you never hurt someone else in the process.

When Is It Okay to Stop Using Trickery on Someone?

Even while manipulation has a lot of power, there are situations in which you shouldn't use it at all. You'll discover that individuals cannot be coerced into doing anything against their will. There is no way to persuade someone adamantly opposed to agreeing with you and carrying out what you are asking them to do without resorting to manipulation techniques, frequently regarded as harsh, aggressive, and abusive.

To become an expert manipulator, you must practice maintaining sensitive boundaries and developing the appropriate techniques without endangering the other person. There will be instances where the victim tells you no, and it is your responsibility as the manipulator to accept that. Naturally, this does not imply that you have to give up entirely; you can continue to use persuasive techniques to see if you can naturally persuade the other person to change their mind. You shouldn't, however, attempt to persuade someone else to alter their thoughts or viewpoint. The idea of manipulation starts to become harmful and should be avoided when you try to impose your beliefs on the other person.

How Can I Identify Disguise?

While most of us won't resort to unethical means to ensure our demands are met, we all want to ensure they are. On the other hand, a manipulator will gladly use indirect and dishonest methods or aggressive methods to subtly sway someone. These manipulators frequently give off the impression of polite, amiable, and skilled flatterers. Although they are skilled at making the other person feel significant, the manipulator uses this technique to further their agenda.

However, manipulation can also go the other way. They may tend to utilize aggression and abuse more to get what they desire. When this occurs, the person's primary goal is to acquire power rather than accomplish other goals. The victim may not even know they are deliberately intimidated in certain situations.

A manipulator has several tools at their disposal, and they are not hesitant to use as many of them as it takes to physically assist them. They could employ foot-in-the-door tactics, reversals, evasiveness, empathy, excuses, feigned worry, comparison, denial, whining, acting naive or naïve, and much more.

No matter how shady the means they employ to achieve their goals, the manipulator won't feel bad about utilizing it to their benefit. Certain manipulators will contest any precise promises they made, any agreements struck, or even the existence of any communication. They may also hold their victim accountable for actions they did not take to acquire sympathy or influence. This strategy is employed to violate a contract, a commitment, and a deadline. When parents engage in bribery, you could even witness manipulation of this kind—for example, "finish your dinner to get dessert."

Another thing to be aware of when manipulating someone is that they will frequently make assumptions about your goals and beliefs and then act as though they were correct. They use this as one justification for their behavior or emotions. They will keep denying the victim's statements made during the conversation at the same time. To help squash any concerns you might have about the circumstance, the manipulator may pretend that something has been settled upon or agreed upon when it hasn't.

After this modest request comes actual demand, which is typically far more, given that they have already agreed to the first request, the victim might find it more difficult to refuse this second one. The manipulator is prepared to step in and take on the role of the person who was offended if the victim does attempt to refuse the second request. In an attempt to persuade the victim to do what they like, they will fabricate a substantial amount of the victim's remarks and ensure that they are the ones who suffer the consequences. Even though the victim had been willing to assist with the initial request, they are very good at making it seem like the issue is about them and their concerns, which puts the victim on the defensive.

Another tactic many manipulators use to achieve their goals is to appear concerned. Because the manipulator is prepared to warn and worry about the victim, this strategy effectively undermines the victim's confidence and decision-making.

Emotional blackmail is something else you may look for in manipulators. The manipulator may resort to anger, threats, guilt, and shame to get the victim to do what they want. Shaming is a useful tactic since it can induce self-doubt in the victim and make them feel extremely anxious about their actions or words. The embarrassment will frequently be concealed under a flattering statement such as, "It's surprising that you, of all people, would stoop to that!" Sometimes, a blackmailer will use anger management techniques to intimidate their target into sacrificing their own needs and desires. Should this prove ineffective, the manipulator may become irrationally irate instead of terrifying. The victim will recognize the difference and consent to do anything the manipulator requests because they are relieved by the change.

Additionally, keep an eye out for behavior referred to as passive-aggressive. When you find it difficult to say no to someone, you could consent to do things you don't want to do to obtain what you want, like neglecting to accomplish something, being late, or only giving it your all. Passive aggressiveness is typically used to express hostility, either on your part or that of the manipulator. You can conveniently avoid doing something you didn't want to do in the first place and get even with your partner by purposefully forgetting.

Of course, we occasionally act in this way without recognizing it. Perhaps we forget to do something because we don't think it's important enough to remember. We don't aim to injure the other person, yet sometimes it happens unintentionally. However, the manipulator will go a step further and attempt to persuade the target to do what they want or avoid doing something they don't want to by obligingly neglecting to complete the task at hand or performing it improperly.

As you can see, there will be a wide variety of sizes and forms for manipulators. Since manipulators frequently wear multiple hats and you are frequently close to the beginning, it can be difficult to determine whether you agree with one or not. A manipulator isn't going to appear out of nowhere one day in your life. You know that these total strangers may take some time to earn your trust. The majority of the time, those who manipulate you are those who are close to you—friends, relatives, or even coworkers.

The first measures to protect yourself are to become aware of the warning signals of manipulation and to ask yourself the correct questions to determine whether manipulation is occurring. Avoiding the manipulator if you know what is happening and can voice your concerns early on will be simpler. The goal of manipulators is to achieve their goals. The manipulator will look for someone else if the target of their manipulation is putting up a strong struggle or has discovered what they are up to.

Memories gone bad (exploding)

There are excellent experiences and unpleasant experiences in life. Every one of these encounters is preserved in a memory device. While the positive memories help you to reminisce about the wonderful times, the negative memories frequently cause anxiety. Furthermore, if a negative memory is consistently brought up in your subconscious, it develops into a "chronic" fear that could eventually become a pattern. Forty-two people (21 women and 21 men) participated in a clinical trial that Pourmansour conducted in 1997. Pourmansour used

NLP to treat the dental treatment fright that each of these people was experiencing. Before the trial, he used a state-fear questionnaire to gauge their degree of phobia. He conducted one collapse-anchor session lasting two hours. He saw a substantial decline in his patient's level of dental fear.

For a group, Huflejt-Lukasik M modified a brief neuro-linguistic therapy session. His goal was to make the group feel uncomfortable in public. He used the SKNS to gauge their self-consciousness before conducting a once-weekly monthly session. He saw a decrease in the group's social anxiety after the month.

Experiences get ingrained in your brain, so waking up one morning and erasing bad memories is challenging.

The most effective method for eliminating unpleasant memories is to apply NLP . Some methods will encourage you to ignore or pretend that your negative memories don't exist (because they do, why deceive yourself?).

NLP teaches you how to effectively handle and replace negative memories with positive ones. Furthermore, NLP will teach you how to access your subconscious and bring up painful memories without feeling overpowered by emotion. You will then be able to look back on your past trauma in a detached manner and draw lessons from it.

Even if unpleasant memories aren't always awful, how you interpret them greatly impacts you. Bad memories can reverberate like ghosts when you perceive them negatively. Your negative recollections "get the best of you" because of the connected memories you have of them. If you look closely, the emotional baggage associated with a negative experience is not all that different from what you experienced in the past when you think back on it.

Then, how can negative memories be erased?

NLP offers a systematic approach that you can utilize to eliminate unpleasant memories. The approach is as follows:

Select A Particular Negative Recollection: Selecting a particularly awful memory to suppress is the first step in utilizing NLP to eliminate negative memories. You'll be able to concentrate your efforts and succeed more. Which unpleasant memory do you wish to let go of?

Establish a Safe Anchor: You must activate a safe anchor as the next step. You can feel comfortable and at ease by setting off a safe anchor. It will also allow you to remember a particular unpleasant experience without being tense or nervous. You must first be in a secure setting before recalling when you felt safe to activate a safe anchor. Once the secure memory is in your subconscious, attach it kinesthetically using your submodalities.

Imagine a blank screen: Once you've established a safe anchor, visualize a blank screen in front of you. Imagine that you are there, and visualize that your image is static.

Bring Back A Negative Memory:

Relax and think about a painful memory that you would like to erase.

Use your submodalities to clarify the particular memory by returning it to mind.

Think of this horrible experience as an observer rather than as a victim when you think back on it.

You can visualize this unpleasant recollection on an imaginary screen in your mind if you start to feel overtaken by emotions. You will free yourself from all emotional attachments to these horrific memories by doing this.

Recalling a negative incident from your past as a younger self is another method to dissociately recall a terrible memory. The notion that "I am wiser and older now" will let you keep an eye on the bad memory from a safe distance.

Take action: Picture yourself entering a negative situation and supporting the younger version of yourself. The purpose of this deed is to let your younger self know that you have changed. Consequently, the impact that remembering your experience has on you will be eliminated.

Future Velocity: Combine the self-image you have of yourself now with the empowered younger version of yourself that is displayed on a screen. The second stage is to revisit the negative memory in your subconscious after you have completed this. Are you still afraid? Does it still give you trouble? Should it occur, you will have to go over each step again.

NLP Anchors

A stimulus known as an anchor helps us relive specific feelings, experiences, and behaviors. One instance of a very powerful anchor is music. When you hear a song, you might be reminded of a certain occasion or a phase of your life. A perfume's aroma may bring back memories of a friend, relative, or former partner who wore it. NLP anchors are essential connections that your brain makes between external stimuli.

Some connections are lovely and sentimental. You can bring yourself back to joyful memories by playing upbeat music or diffusing pleasant aromas throughout your home. However, not all associations are created equal. They evoke horrible memories along with all the suffering connected to them. NLP teaches you how to program yourself to generate new anchors that cause you to feel and act in particular ways and release negative anchors.

You can indeed make your anchors. Because they are so strong, anchors can help you modify your behavior. You must identify a desirable condition for yourself, like motivation or contentment, to develop an anchor. Recall moments when you experienced genuine, enigmatic joy or ecstasy. This may have been your wedding day or the first time you held your newborn. That may have been when you were a child opening presents. You might also think back to instances when you felt accomplished, like taking a challenging college or high school exam.

Next, you need to locate a distinct stimulus that will impact your memory, like a tone or sound that particularly appeals to you. You might even only apply the tactile sense of pressing your thumb and fingers together or your hands together. As you allow your emotions to peak at the memory, picture yourself in the desired state and expose yourself to the stimulation. Get up and do something different to "break" the trance before the sensation disappears. Never allow the emotion or condition to gradually diminish over time. To establish the association, you can do this as many as necessary.

You can employ the stimulus at any time to relive the desired feeling once the link has been established. Simply push your thumb and forefinger together or listen to music to become motivated to pass an exam. Play a pleasant song or engage in any other stimulating activity if you're feeling low and want to cheer yourself up.

Frequent use keeps this anchor from wearing out and helps to solidify it. A robust anchor will endure for a considerable amount of time, but occasionally, you will need to use it to renew it. To maintain your anchors' durability and power, make sure you utilize them all frequently.

What does this signify?

It implies that you should focus just as much on your speech preparation as on your demeanor when preparing for a meeting, presentation, or interview. If you do not monitor your actions closely, you could severely harm your prospects of being heard, obtaining employment, or completing a transaction.

You should also think about how nonverbal cues may impact you personally. A first date is a prime example. When two attracted individuals go on their first date, they can show each other who they are and let the other decide whether or not they would make a good partner. Everyone on a date wants to appear their best.

However, contradictory signals or messages could mislead one or both parties. This could cause an attempt to build a relationship to fall through since the message isn't clear enough.

Think about this:

Even if they might be, a lack of smile and poor posture can indicate that one person is not interested in the other. This demonstrates the sensitivity of body language. However, smiling or making too much physical contact could make one uncomfortable.

Of course, it's crucial to strike a balance so that verbal cues, physical touch, body language, and visual contact make sense. In this book, it is what we are aiming for. To equip you with the necessary resources to successfully communicate your message.

Visual contact is another essential component of communication. This kind of contact—also known as "eye contact"—is essential when attempting to interact with others.

Making too much eye contact could be interpreted as aggressive, while making too little eye contact could be interpreted as mysterious and cause your interlocutor to get uncomfortable. Maintaining good eye contact will help you come out as sincere and real. Conversely, your communication will be relatable and relevant because of your ability to speak with your eyes.

Consider making a public address.

Your audience might think you did not convey a moral message if you do not look them in the eye. They might think you were merely going through the motions or your message was not sincere and real. If you can't establish a connection with them, they might just brush off your entire speech.

Furthermore, the most effective public presenters can address a crowd while giving the impression that they are speaking to each person directly. The mastery of this ability takes time. The good news is that you can become an expert at it independently. You don't have to be incredibly talented. With enough effort and commitment, anyone can learn to become proficient in these talents.

Making eye contact is important during negotiations. If you make no eye contact, your rival might feel more confident and try to take the lead in the negotiation. Making too much eye contact could make the other person feel threatened and distant. You won't obtain the desired results in either scenario.

But, you may win the other person's trust by making balanced eye contact, smiling, and maintaining a firm posture. Although doing this alone won't guarantee you achieve the desired outcomes, it will put you in the correct direction.

In terms of relationships, maintaining eye contact is essential when going on a date or just attempting to get along with coworkers, classmates, and business acquaintances. This will demonstrate your friendliness and willingness to contribute positively to a team. This is why making eye contact is important for getting along with others.

The examples given in this chapter demonstrate the different levels of communication that occur. On a conscious level, meaning is mostly communicated through language. The things you say come first at this conscious level.

Your actions, body language, and eye contact convey the strongest message of all on a deeper, more primal level. When used effectively, nonverbal communication can accelerate the delivery of your message. However, if you make a mistake in your nonverbal communication, your message will lose its impact.

Even though most experts concur that nonverbal cues account for over 95% of communication, it's important to balance what you say and how you present yourself. Consequently, the goal of this work is to maximize our existing understanding of nonverbal communication. It is imperative to emphasize that using the appropriate words will propel you forward in your endeavors; the truth is, we don't give a damn about what you say. How you express yourself worries us much more.

Furthermore, our primary goal in this book is to provide you with the fundamental principles that will enable you to create the persona that will allow you to succeed without the need for any devious means. In actuality, all it takes to discover the keys to communicating effectively is understanding the fundamentals of human nature.

Each of the topics we have covered in this book will be covered in more detail in the following chapters.

It's also critical to remember that mastering all the techniques and methods this book covers takes time. Your first few attempts won't go as well unless you have some sort of innate talent for communication. However, you'll discover that building close, personal relationships with others gets simpler with time. As a result, you won't need to consider your possible interactions too much in complete contrast. You'll find that using the methods described in this chapter comes naturally to you.

www.ingramcontent.com/pod-product-compliance
Lightning Source LLC
Chambersburg PA
CBHW052144110526
44591CB00012B/1848